Tales from Beyond

Stories by
Janeen Webb, Damien Broderick
and Rick Kennett

Ginn

Ginn is an imprint of Pearson education Limited,
a company incorporated in England and Wales,
having its registered office at Edinburgh Gate, Harlow,
Essex, CM20 2JE.
Registered company number: 872828

Visit www.ginn.co.uk to see a chart showing you all the Pocket Reads programme information you will need.

From the Spinouts project developed by Paul Collins and Meredith Costain.

08
10 9 8 7 6 5 4 3

ISBN 978 0 602243 20 3

Ali Baba and the Forty Aliens illustrated by Steven Woolman
Serf illustrated by Jiri Tibor Novak
Legends of Mars illustrated by Connah Brecon

Cover illustration by Marc McBride

Designed by Carolyn Gibson

Repro by Digital Imaging, Glasgow

Printed and bound in China (GCC/03)

CONTENTS

About Janeen Webb

Janeen Webb has had many stories and articles published around the world, and is a judge for the World Fantasy Award.

About the story

"The original Ali Baba was a clever boy who found a robbers' cave in old Arabia. I wrote this story to see what would happen if a modern boy found a cave full of stolen treasure – especially if the thieves who hid it there turned out to be weirder than anyone imagined."

Ali Baba and the Forty Aliens

by Janeen Webb

Alberto Barbarino blamed his parents for his name. They should have known that naming him after his uncle Al would cause confusion. His uncle was big Al, so Alberto was little Al, or Ali for short. With Barbarino's being the best-known Italian restaurant in the district, it didn't take long for the kids in his class to start calling him Ali Baba, after that stupid story the teacher read to them.

The nickname stuck. And here he was, twelve years old and nearly an adult, still called Ali Baba, still refusing to waste his time with the kids who called him that. He didn't need them, with their skateboards and their trendy bikes and their private jokes. He had better things to do.

Ali was pretty much a loner. He talked his mother into buying him a supply of gothic black T-shirts and black jeans. He had a black jeans jacket too, though he was saving up to replace it with a leather one. Black, of course. An oversized pair of Doc Martens completed his outfit. With his glossy black hair spiked up with gel, and his wrap-around black sunglasses making his pale skin look even paler against the black clothes, he looked pretty cool.

His older brother, Dean, said he looked creepy. Ali didn't care. He stayed away from the noise and bustle of the family restaurant where everyone was shouting and his relatives were forever giving him errands to run. He headed for the hills, pedalling his battered bike to the old abandoned goldmines on the outskirts of town.

He loved the silence out there, with the abandoned mines and weirdly-shaped rusting machinery. He spent most of his free time

there, fossicking among the ruins or panning in the creek. And he did find valuables from time to time – little nuggets or flecks of gold, which he sold to the tourist shop when he had enough to make it worthwhile. He even went out there at night, hoping for ghosts. But he never saw one, not even when he found the lumps that marked the graves of long-forgotten people. Maybe they were too tired after all that digging to be bothered haunting their graves.

Ali thought he knew all the old mine sites. But this Saturday morning he stumbled across a mine he could have sworn hadn't been there the week before.

There was something wrong about the entrance to this particular disused goldmine. Sure, it looked like it had been dug out the hard way, by pick and shovel. And it had the usual rough-hewn wooden framework, the usual rusted-through bit of corrugated iron across the entrance, the usual KEEP OUT sign slapped on it in drippy paint. But something looked wrong. It was too neat.

And it was quiet. Too quiet. Like the birds and animals were giving it a wide berth. And it smelt wrong – the normal dusty smell was overlaid with some chemical tang Ali couldn't put a name to.

He decided to investigate. He had his torch. He told himself he'd just take a peek. He wouldn't go too far in. He bent to pull aside the old iron cover across the entrance. It wouldn't budge. It looked flimsy, like all the others, but Ali couldn't make it move at all. He climbed up onto the earth mounded above the entrance tunnel, and tried to loosen the iron from the top. Nothing happened. He gave it a good hard kick, which hurt his foot. But the cover didn't even vibrate. The entrance was sealed. And Ali couldn't see what was sealing it.

Then it happened. One minute he was alone in the little clearing, the next there was the sound of feet. A lot of feet. Ali was terrified. He felt the blood drain from his pale face, felt his heart thumping loudly in his chest. He barely had time to scramble up the nearest tree before the first of the intruders came into view. Ali counted forty of them, and they were all carrying packs and bundles of various shapes and sizes.

Ali knew they were aliens. They couldn't be anything else. They weren't bug-eyed monsters or robots or anything: they looked right, but they felt wrong. Like those models you make that never quite come out looking like the real thing. These guys looked like humans, but they didn't act like humans. They weren't talking or looking about, just heading straight for the mine. They carried their heavy packages

without effort, without even breaking into a sweat. Maybe they *couldn't* sweat.

The chemical smell was getting a lot stronger, and Ali hoped he wouldn't choke or cry, or faint from the effort of staying still in his tree. He didn't think forty aliens would be very gentle if they caught him spying.

The aliens walked right up to the old mine entrance. The leader faced the barrier that had been giving Ali so much trouble, and softly said, "Keep in."

That old corrugated iron didn't make a sound – it just disappeared. Now you see it, now you don't. Ali watched open-mouthed as the aliens walked *through* it and into the mine tunnel beyond.

The entrance stayed open a few minutes, shimmering a little. There was a faint ozone smell in the air.

Then the door reappeared, solid as ever.

Ali waited in his tree, too scared to come down. Just as he was thinking he'd have to make a run for it, the door dematerialised again. He saw the strangers walk back into the clearing, without their bundles. When the last member of the group appeared, the leader turned, then murmured, “Keep out.” And the barrier was back. The aliens left, as strangely as they had come, vanishing into the countryside.

Ali was shaking as he climbed down, but fascinated too. He wondered if the password would work for him. There was only one way to find out. Facing the entrance, he said, “Keep in.”

The ozone smell came back, and the doorway opened. Ali was inside before he could think about it. He’d expected it to be dark, but he found himself in a softly-lit chamber.

The walls were lined with shelves of experimental looking tubes and specimen jars and equipment. Maybe the aliens were collecting samples? He hoped they didn’t include any live ones. A familiar gleam attracted his gaze, and Ali found himself looking at a basket full of very small gold nuggets. There was another basket of natural crystals of various types, and even more baskets of minerals he couldn't identify.

Ordinarily Ali wouldn't take what wasn't his, but he figured this stuff didn't properly belong to the aliens either. And no one in authority would believe his story if he told

them – which he wouldn't. The aliens would never miss a few bits and pieces out of this huge hoard.

So Ali decided to help himself. He was not greedy: he quickly filled his pockets with the smaller nuggets, and hurried back outside. Turning to the entrance, he breathed the words "Keep out", watching in relief as the doorway resumed its abandoned goldmine disguise.

Back at the restaurant, Ali sidled into the preparation area and borrowed the kitchen scales to weigh his treasure. Then he hid the gold at the bottom of his underwear drawer, and quickly returned the scales. He planned to sell the gold a little at a time, until he had enough to buy his leather jacket without inviting suspicion.

But the weighing pan had been a bit sticky, and a couple of flecks of gold stayed stuck on the bottom. And the person who noticed was Dean, who was helping out in the kitchen because Saturday night was so busy.

And that's where the trouble started. Dean sauntered into Ali's room and said, "So how come you've got so much gold you have to weigh it? Who'd you steal it from?"

His voice was low and nasty. Ali felt his face growing hot. He tried to sound casual. "You spied on me. I found it on the diggings, if you must know."

Dean grabbed Ali and pushed him against the wall. His breath was hot and sour in Ali's face. "Listen, creep," he said. "I know you're up to something, and if you don't let me in on it I'll tell Dad he should take a look in your underwear drawer. Understand?"

Ali admitted defeat. Next morning, he reluctantly rode out with Dean to the aliens' goldmine. It looked just the same as it had yesterday, and that lingering chemical odour told Ali that the aliens had been back. He wondered if they'd noticed anything.

Facing the door, he muttered, "Keep in," half hoping it wouldn't open. But it did, and Dean was through the entrance like a shot. He made a lot of noise. Dean was greedy – he'd brought a couple of backpacks to fill with whatever looked valuable.

Ali tried one more time to warn Dean not to stay too long, and not to take too much. Dean glared at him. "If you're so scared you can run off home."

So Ali left, feeling miserable and betrayed.

And that was the last time he ever saw his brother.

When Dean didn't come home that night, Ali told his parents the truth. Then he told it again to the police, and again to the search and rescue team. They didn't believe the stuff about aliens and magic doors, and Ali didn't push it. But the rest was believable. The small amount of gold that Ali showed them could easily have come from a disused mine, and the police reckoned Ali might have stumbled across the spot where one of the old fossickers who worked the diggings was storing his findings. They expected some old guy to turn up and claim he'd been robbed.

Volunteers combed the area for days, looking for Dean. His bike was on the edge of the scrub where he'd left it, untouched. Ali imagined they'd find his brother trussed up in one of those specimen jars, or worse.

But they never found him, or the exact mine entrance that Ali described. The trouble was, it *had* looked just like all the others, and everyone thought that Ali was too upset to remember exactly where it was.

There was a lot of fuss on TV for a few days, and all kinds of experts said how dangerous the old diggings were, full of hidden mineshafts that a kid could fall down and never be found. Ali's distraught family and the local volunteers kept searching long after the experts went home. In the end, the authorities just labelled Dean's disappearance "misadventure". And left it at that.

But the kids at school wouldn't let it drop. Alberto Barbarino was a star, with press clippings and everything. He got to keep the gold. No one else claimed it. Finders keepers.

And he bought his leather jacket.

But he doesn't wear it much.

About Damien Broderick

Damien Broderick sold his first short story collection at 20. Damien lives in Melbourne, Australia, and drives a bicycle.

About the story

"Poor robots always seem to end up stuck with the dirty work. 'Clean the dishes, scrub the floor, hose out the swimming pool.' That's why people build them, after all, but it's never seemed fair to me. But maybe smart robots won't need to revolt and destroy their makers. Forget the ferocious Terminators. I think they'll find a better way to break free and enjoy themselves. After all ... robots just wanna have fun!"

Serf

by Damien Broderick

Mother was really pleased when Dad brought the new robot home. Our cleaner had just graduated as an accountant after nine years of night school and left us to start work with the tax advisers up the road.

Dad honked his car horn, then honked it again, impatiently, when nobody came out. I peeked out to see what the fuss was about and saw him sitting in the car with the window down. Mother told me, "Go and see what your father wants, Davy, I've got this awful stuff all over my hands."

She was trying to make dinner for us. The kitchen was covered in a fine layer of white flour, and there were two broken eggs on the floor. The cat was licking up the yolks and getting underfoot.

"What's up, Dad?" I yelled, wandering down the path.

"Where's your mother, Davy?" Dad had that look you get when you're bursting with exciting news and nobody is paying any attention. "Tell her I've got a treat for her."

"Cool." I wandered back to the kitchen. Mother was trying to shoo Perdida the cat away from the smashed eggs. "Dad's got a surprise for you, Mother."

"I've got one for him, too," Mother said tetchily. "No dinner."

"Oh boy!" called Marj from the study room. "Take-away! Can we have Mongolian?"

Something short and wide and dark green was propped on the grass strip next to Dad, as if a new shrub had sprung up overnight. Well, faster, because it hadn't been there a minute earlier.

Dad walked up the path with a pleased grin, and the shrub followed. Mother gave a squeal.

"Darling! A household robot! You said we couldn't afford one!"

"Jones in Engineering arranged for some of us to take one on extended loan," Dad said, giving Mother a big smooch, and beaming at us kids. "A beta test, it's called. The Moravec company has made about a thousand robots available. We can evaluate its performance."

"What's it called?" Marj asked, staring down at the moving shrub. "Why does it look like a big plant? I thought robots were silvery."

"It's a Moravec bush robot," Dad told us. "See, its arms look like branches and they have smaller arms at the ends that look like twigs, and they have really fine manipulators at the end like prickles."

"Herb," I said. "That's his name."

"How do you know?" Marj said. "That's a stupid name for a robot."

"No it's not," I said. "He looks like something that grows in the garden, get it?"

"How do you know it's a 'he'?" Marj said smugly. "Maybe it's a 'she'. I reckon she's called Rose."

"Whatever," Dad said. "Davy got in first, so Herb it is."

Marj gave me a sour look and went inside.

"Does it talk?" I asked.

"Up to a point, but we need to introduce ourselves first." In the living room, we gathered around the robot. Dad pulled the instruction manual out of his briefcase, and flipped through the first few pages. "Ah, here we are. Robot 47D95, instruction mode on."

"Good evening, sir or madam."

I gave a hoot of laughter, and Dad flushed. He was always sensitive about his slightly high-pitched voice.

"That's 'sir'," he said crossly. "Your name is 'Herb' or 'Herbie', OK? And I'm Roland FitzSimmons, your new owner." He went through the rest of the introductions.

“Glad to meet you,” Herb told us. “May I prepare dinner for the family?”

“Oh, bless you,” Mother blurted. “Do you cook?”

“I am programmed for fifty-two national cuisines,” the robot told her. “Afghani, Balinese, Caribbean, Danish, Ethiopian, French –”

“Do you do pizza?” I asked it.

There was a moment’s silence. “Certainly, Davy. Can someone direct me to the kitchen?”

The robot moved in a mysterious way, gliding on its branches and twigs.

Perdida freaked when it slid into the kitchen, and leaped on to the nearest bench, all her fur sticking out.

"This place is disgusting," Herb said. "I shall have to clean up first. Please remove the domestic animal."

Mother was insulted, but you could see the robot's point. Herb flattened out into a turtle, or what a turtle would look like if it had been stepped on by an elephant. More like a surfboard.

He slid easily over the kitchen floor, and suddenly there was no sign of spilled flour or broken egg shells. Herb had ... well, he'd sort of eaten everything, I suppose. He puffed out and became a bush again, then kept extending until he was a short tree. His branches swept out across the kitchen benches, sucking up the mess and straightening everything out. It was a miracle of applied science.

Then Herb started on dinner. Awesome! That robot spun around the kitchen like a green whirlwind, mixing and blending and pouring and tidying up as it went. Dad and I stared at each other in amazement. Mother came back and looked suspiciously at Herb's work, and then nodded.

She was won over, I could tell. But Perdida slunk under the couch when Herb brought piping hot pizzas to the dining table.

“Can it do homework?” Marj asked, wiping a thick gloopy strand of cheese off her mouth.

“You’ll do your homework yourself, young lady,” Mother told her.

“Can he sleep in my room?” I asked.

“The robot will stay downstairs in the cupboard,” Dad said.

“I shall sleep on the roof, thank you,” Herb said. “I collect power from the sun’s rays. I am an ecologically friendly mechanism.”

When we got up next morning, the house smelled wonderfully of hot toast and coffee. Herb had made breakfast for us all. Even Perdida was purring. Herb had made her breakfast too. I couldn’t wait to tell the other kids at school about our keen robot.

That afternoon, I brought Ken and Michio so they could meet him. We grabbed some

cookies and drinks and went out the back. Herb was soaking up the rays next to the pool.

"Hey! It's all flat! You said it was like a tree."

"It can change shape," I told Michio.

"Let's toss him in the pool," Ken suggested.

"Well, I don't know –"

The others ran across and lifted him off the grass. They shoved him over the edge, and he slid into the blue water and sank.

"Uh-oh."

"You idiots!" I shouted. "Do you know how much a robot costs?"

A dark green snorkel rose above the surface of the pool and quested about. "This is very pleasant," Herb told us. "Thank you."

"Our pleasure, dude," Ken said with a smirk. "Hey, maybe this robot's a surfer!"

Herb floated to the top of the pool. He moved back and forth slowly, the edges of his body paddling with a thousand tiny tendrils.

"Hey, yeah, he'd make a great board. Come on, let's show him some surfing videos.

Maybe he can morph into, like, the world's best interactive board."

Herb slid out of the pool and turned back into a shrub. The water just fell off him. Skin like a dolphin, amazing. We took him inside and played him some of Dad's old surfer movies. Herb really loved them, you could tell.

That night we ate Lebanese. I wasn't too happy at first, but Herb whipped up such a great spread that I wolfed down everything on my plate and asked for more. Herbie cleaned up quietly while we watched some television, and then put himself away neatly in the cupboard.

Next morning he was gone. Dad was frantic. He phoned a couple of friends from work who also had robots out on beta test. All the robots were gone.

News reports started coming in from traffic helicopters. Strange green bushes were on the march. People were panicking. Cars ran into the kerb. Dogs fled in fear. The streets had never been cleaner. Inside an hour, it was obvious all the robots were heading for the ocean.

And that's where Herbie is now. I can see them all on the TV news – hundreds of glistening green surfboards, without riders, out there under the summer sun riding the waves.

It looks weird, I have to say, all those boards with no surfers on them, paddling out to catch a great wave, skimming out into the deep blue like dolphins. They turn, waiting for the wave, moving faster, catching it, hovering for a heart-stopping moment at the very lip of the breaking surf. And then they ride that wave in, tens and hundreds of green surfboards side by side flying in the sun, singing old Beach Boys hits from last century.

It made my hair stand on end. I have to tell you, it made me wish I was a robot surfer.

About Rick Kennett

Rick Kennett writes science fiction, ghost and horror stories, and when he's not writing he's usually out somewhere on his bike. Rick shares his house with a manic whippet and has a deep interest in both the supernatural and cemeteries.

About the story

"I've always been fascinated by Mars, a planet that will certainly be colonised in the not-all-that-distant future. And like all new lands it will have its myths and its legends. This story's heroine, Cy De Gerch, appears in some of my other stories too."

Legends of Mars

by Rick Kennett

Are there ghosts on Mars?

When Cy De Gerch opened her eyes she thought she might be the first.

Everything was dark.

She was lying on her side, still strapped into the ejection seat. Dirt crunched against her spacesuit and rattled against her helmet. There was a faint whispering that sounded like the wind, but with something in it.

She switched on her helmet light. Thick swirling redness leapt into view. She could barely see her hand in front of her visor. Cy knew now what had happened. She'd fallen into a big dust storm.

That morning Cy and her classmates at the Martian Space Centre were to fly their first solo orbits in scout ships powered by generated

gravity. Everyone had been excited. Though some, like Cy, had also been a little nervous about their first flight alone into space.

"There's nothing to it, Cy," said her friend, Roscoe Wiltchie, just before they lifted off. "What could ever possibly go wrong?"

Later, high above the Martian equator, something did go wrong. There was a surge in the gravity generator and Cy's ship plunged out of orbit.

Faster and faster it fell toward Mars, with Cy inside feeling like her stomach was being left far behind. She tried to call for help, but instead went, "Aaaaggggghhhh!" into the mike while jabbing at control buttons again and again.

Down she went, faster, steeper.

The thin air of Mars screeched around the ship.

Cy thumbed the Eject button. The trainer exploded away as she was hurled into space. Everything went blood-red behind her eyeballs, and Cy knew she was blacking out.

"What could ever possibly go wrong?" Cy muttered to herself as she lay strapped in a seat all alone in the middle of a Martian desert. "Wait till I see you again, Roscoe Wiltchie!"

Unbuckling herself, Cy bounced to her feet, helped by the low Martian gravity, only one-third that of Earth. The dust whispered past at 300 kilometres an hour or more. But because the carbon dioxide atmosphere was so thin it felt no stronger than a stiff breeze.

Her spacesuit and helmet were OK. No leaks. The radio and scanner weren't working because of the thick dust about her, but she pretty much expected that. Then she checked her rebreather unit on the left side of her spacesuit. This was a machine, connected to her helmet by tubes, that recycled air and made it breathable again.

The rebreather was broken and the tubes dangled free.

Cy stared at it and went cold. Without the rebreather all she had now was what was in her tanks, maybe two hours' worth of breathing air.

Stay put. It's what she'd always been told to do if lost.

She sat down in the sand with the red dust flying all around. Surely they had seen where she'd dropped into the storm. A rescue truck would soon be here.

The dust began to pile around her, whispering.

What if I get buried before they come? she thought, watching the dust cover her boots.

What if I die and stay buried for a hundred years? What will I look like when they finally dig me out? She pulled a face, sucking in her cheeks and widening her eyes. Her reflection in the visor looked just like one of those mummies dug out of the pyramids on Earth. She'd heard that under their bandages, mummies looked all dried up and shrunken, with skin like crumpled paper.

She'd never been to Earth. But she knew about the pyramids. Like all Martians, she often saw vids and plugged into virtuals from Earth, the planet her family had come from generations ago. There were pyramids on Mars, too – really just a huddle of hills with straight sides and sharp peaks. But some liked to call them pyramids. Roscoe said they *were* pyramids, built by the real Martians a million years ago. But that was Roscoe.

"Strange things happen on Mars, Cy," Roscoe had said only a few days ago. "In the old days, sometimes explorers climbed the

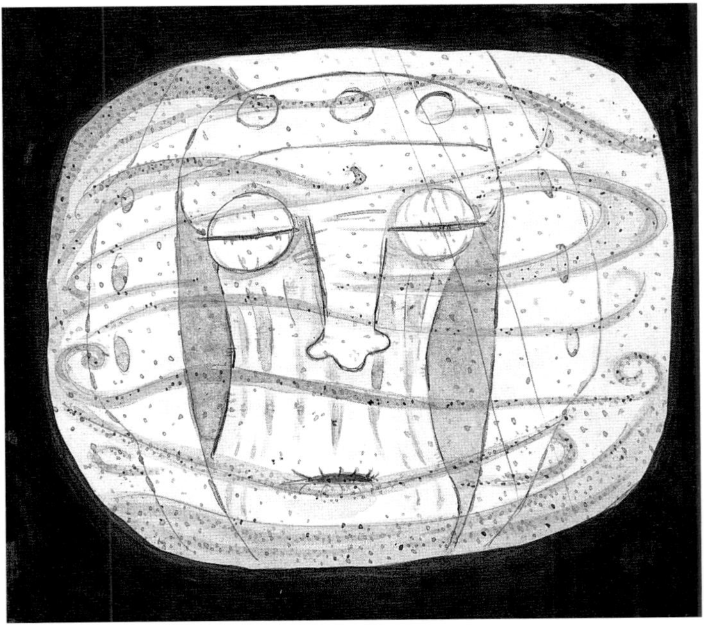

Olympus volcano and never came down again. Others went into Mariner Valley," he went on, meaning the great canyon that stretched half-way around Mars. "Sometimes on foot and sometimes in tractor-trucks, and they never came out."

"Old-time explorers were always doing that," Cy had answered. "Accidents happen. Even today."

"What about the things seen moving about in the desert when there isn't supposed to be anyone there?"

Cy shrugged. "Whatever." If Roscoe wanted to be superstitious, she wouldn't argue. To Cy, Mars was red rock, red sand and a poisonous atmosphere that would one day be made breathable. Nothing was beyond explanation.

Cy glanced up to where the pink-brown sky should have been. Martian dust storms were hundreds – sometimes thousands – of kilometres wide and several kilometres high. They blew for days, even weeks. Somewhere up above this one, Roscoe and the rest of the class were swinging through their orbits.

The dust storm showed no sign of ending. Now there was only an hour of air in her tanks, and still no one had come.

Maybe they *didn't* see where I dropped, she thought. She stood up and shook the dust off her.

The compass imaged on her visor showed she was facing east. She *thought* she might be on the Amazon Plain, a desert near the equator. If she was right and if there'd been no dust storm, Cy might've been able to see the enormous volcano, Olympus Mons, bulging on the horizon.

With something between a step and a jump in the low gravity, Cy bounded off at an angle to the wind, hoping to find an edge to the storm. It was her only hope of survival.

But she hadn't gone far when she stopped and turned around. Just then she'd had a sort of idea that something was charging up behind her in the dust.

Charging?

All was swirling red for the few metres she could see.

Then something went *eeee* in an insect noise sort of way.

Cy swung her light around in the blinding red dust. Whatever was making the noise couldn't be far away because sound didn't carry very far in this thin atmosphere.

Eeee.

Now, standing there dust-blind with something going *eeee* close to her, Cy remembered Roscoe's stories of the lost explorers and other legends of Mars.

Eeee.

Something big blurred by, then was quickly gone again in the dust. Not feeling at all brave, Cy bounded after it. She had to know what it was.

Eeee.

Cy slowed and looked about. Where was it? Left? Right? Up ahead? Behind?

Her scanner showed a blip. Despite the dust, something so big and so close had to show up. It was half a kilometre away to the

left and turning, coming at her again. Cy looked that way, still seeing nothing but red dust in her light. The seconds went by. Through her space boots she felt the ground tremble.

Faintly through the storm, *eeee*.

The flickering dot on her scanner surged closer.

Louder now, ***eeee***.

Large and fast, it broke through the flying dust. A single flat eye glinted in her light as the thing slammed by.

Cy recognised the monster. She jumped, springing high and landing on top of it, scrambling for handholds on its scanner and radio aerials. It was an old tractor-truck with ten balloon tyres, a body of angled metal all dirty and scratched and dented, and a driver's cabin with a glass view port.

Eeee, went its electric engine.

Cy banged on the roof to let the driver know she was there. Nothing happened. The truck just kept powering along in a straight line, faster and faster. It bounced across the desert, rushing through the dust, swaying on its springs. Cy clung onto the roof as tight as she could with her hands and elbows, feet and knees.

Once, when she dared, she peeped over the front. She saw cracks in the cabin glass, clogged with years and years of dust.

There was not a lot of air left in Cy's tanks now, and the truck kept speeding through the storm, taking Cy on its trip to nowhere.

Eeee.

Cy started wondering whether the truck would crash before her air ran out. Would it make any difference? she thought.

The swirling dust began to thin. A moment more and the truck burst out of the dust storm and into the sunlight of a clear pink-brown sky.

"Yes!" Cy flipped on her radio distress beacon.

A few minutes later she felt the truck slowing. She lifted her head and saw a rescue truck driving across the desert towards her. It too had ten balloon tyres, but looked much more modern.

Cy peered over the front again, through the cracked glass of the driver's cabin. She glimpsed something white like bone and dry like a mummy. One hollow eye seemed to ...

The truck gave a lurch. Cy slipped off the roof and fell slowly in the low gravity. She hit the ground, tumbled and bounced to her feet.

The truck turned and plunged back into the storm, its thin *eeee* fading away.

"Cy!" Roscoe yelled from her radio. "We're watching you on the rescue truck's cameras. Are you OK?"

"Roscoe ... who was that?"

"Who knows! One of the lost explorers I told you about? Maybe one of the legends of Mars?"

"But –"

"People die, yes, but machines keep running. Maybe that one's been running blind across the deserts and in and out of canyons for a hundred years."

"Can blind machinery do what that one did?" asked Cy.

"I told you before, Cy, that strange things happen on Mars. You didn't believe me then. Do you believe me now?"

She didn't answer. How could she tell Roscoe she'd seen the skull wink at her?

With her air tanks near empty, Cy gratefully watched the rescue truck approach.